Monk Eats an Afro

Monk Eats an Afro

Yolanda Wisher

Hanging Loose Press
Brooklyn, New York

For Theo

Trial and error loss and gain
It takes some doing
Monkery's a slow slow train

—"Blue Monk," Thelonious Monk (music)
Abbey Lincoln (lyrics)

TABLE OF CONTENTS

I   THE MYTH OF STEW

II   SLOW DRAG

III   HARRIET

IV   MONK EATS AN AFRO

I   THE MYTH OF STEW

.

PEA SONG

Black-eyed peas
Will make a sista mean
Fight ya for em
Till the grass ain't green

Knew a girl named
Black-eyed Sue
She kept the peas in a high-laced shoe

She said
I can't start my new year right
Unless my peas is outta sight

Nana kept em in a pocketbook
Same as Tab & dear Aunt Sook

But Mama kept em in her dresser drawer
Drawls scented with the onion core

Turkey butt pepper Lawry's
Make ya shit out cowries

C'mon
Black-eyed peas
Will make a sista mean

Fight ya for em
Till the grass ain't green

The Myth of Stew

a pot   don't call it a cauldron
could feed millions for eternity

the tree of life could be tasted
shitted out   released into porcelain

her foot   that walked so many miles
could season better than Little Miss Salt Shower

make you forget how Daddy
run off with the check on payday
odds and ends in the fridge

our nigger ambrosia
our promethean fat
our infidel broth

a woman and her girls
sitting at the table
like thick spoons

My Family of Women

raised me to be mouthy and mighty
schooled me with slant looks and girdled grips
made talk like oatmeal to coat my ears against
the lurching of menfolk who would prefer my meat
to Murray's. They stood between me and the precipice.

Church women and pinochle sinners
gave me my tutelage in fatherlessness, their tongues
commanded by a ruthless orgy of verbal desire
broke my mind into seven spheres.

They were good women. With demons
in their pocketbooks. They'd hand me
a tissue or a mint and for a second
that abyss would open,
beckoning.

SOOKIE

my great aunt
squash gourds
for titties

went to Atlantic City monthly
came back with ashtrays
made into ornate vaginas

tossed a head of Jeri curls
sipped molasses black coffee
with rum

told me
menstruation
was regal

said I was a southern gal
had to keep my kootamaya tight
for a real man

had no shame ever
no babies
just her knickknacks

but I swear

in that old wedding picture
her thighs inflamed
in garnet nylons

she look
fertile
as all hell

AUNT TAB'S FUNERAL

woke up this mornin
decided to wear a fuchsia dress
to your final gig
turtleneck, cashmere
belted and snug
I dared some ole biddy
to say somethin
I felt you admirin
my shape
you were always
into shapes
curves
womanly dimensions
that couldn't fit in
a Cousin Vit coffin

the men got in a fight
outside the club
while the old heads
told your
dirty stories
rolled your
flaws in papers
dipped in memoryshine
from the Shenandoah

I saw your shape
Marlboro smoke
round your temples
walkin home
down Maple Street

SONG: CROSSWOMAN BLUES

I went down to the crossroads
Four ways to go
Devil say, "Pick one"
Naturally, I couldn't resist

I came back from the crossroads
With the devil's head in my purse
Singin "Man, any way I choose
Gonna lead me home!"

Next I went lookin for the boogieman's ass
Tired of him keepin my children up at night
Put my foot in his boogie
Gave him somethin to boogie about

I went down to the crossroads
Me & Eshu
Beat the mess outta some baaaad
Spirits in the bush

& then we built a garden
Over their dead bodies
Yeah, we built a garden
Over their dead bodies

See I'm Bessie
& I'm Bigger
I'm Harriet
With iron for mind

John Henry's jinn
Ma Rainey's juicy fruit
Pirate Jenny's conspiracy

& I'm built like a garden
Over their dead bodies
Yeah, I'm built like a garden
Over their dead bodies

Violin to Fiddle

Mom whacked me
with the bow

locked me in her bedroom
to practice
with the shades closed

she had paid
too much money
on a violin
to have me embarrass her
at the third grade recital

on the school lawn springtime
after all the White and Asian kids
grinded out "Perpetual Motion"
Mr. Tackett, the conductor
his glass eye grinning
like an overseer
announced the end
of the program

but my mother stood up
and introduced me
to the crowd herself—

but I hesitated to
move from my seat
insisting it was okay
that he forgot me

my mother wasn't
having it and hissed
    you are Black
    and have a right to this

so I stood up
to play my solo
in my yellow dress
dotted with gray flowers
tiny waves of lace
at the shoulders
a bumblebee found me quick
about three bars in
but I kept on playing
like a can of Raid in that dress

and as the bee sat on my bow
as she buzzed around my ear
I heard her hum:

    you are Black
    and have a right to this

    this be your fiddle
    claim it

Song: Basketball Gypsies

You & me travelin women
Children in our limbs dyin for spring

You & me basketball gypsies
Wearin hoops of golden charm

You & me circus ladies
Shavin beards of wisdom from navel to thigh

Like a guru need disciples
Like the moon need the tide
Like the water need a way
You need me

Like disciples need a guru
Like the tide need the moon
Like the way need water
I need you

You & me wear the same face
Sometimes I wanna wipe it off

You & me so close sometimes
I wonder if I'll suffocate

But you & me leapin from the same trapeze
You & me skydivin hand-in-hand

Like a guru need disciples
Like the moon need the tide
Like the water need a way
You need me

Like disciples need a guru
Like the tide need the moon
Like the way need water
I need you

GOOGLISM FOR MY FATHER, 2005

Jeffrey Johnson is fire chief of rescue
Jeffrey Johnson is chair of the eerie past beyond hearing
Jeffrey Johnson is a responsible fellow of reconfigurational studies
Jeffrey Johnson is outstanding and currently full of shit
Jeffrey Johnson is a choir of glass houses and altar boys
Jeffrey Johnson is pastor of the slam dunk cavalry
Jeffrey Johnson said his couldn't be bought
Jeffrey Johnson is trying to reach out
Jeffrey Johnson is a relocation specialist
Jeffrey Johnson is a professor of complexity
Jeffrey Johnson is rowing toward death
Jeffrey Johnson got next

Song: Ancestors

Ancestors
Where do they go?

Mama say they
Leave their tracks in snow
Papa say they
Trip on light to Milky Way

Become nebulous
In the dark void
Of the mind

She's in the deep, I know
Fathoms between us drift
But do you have to die to swim?

Ancestors
Which way they fly?

Zora say they
Corn-liquor ether
Jimmy say they
Bonfires of the heart

Forging knives of memory
Out of the dark void
Of the mind

She's in the deep, I know
Fathoms between us drift
But do you have to die to swim?

Ancestors
When shall we meet again?

Walt say
In the bubbles of the stew

Pablo say
In the iridescence of fish

Pulled breathless
From the dark void
Of the mind

II   SLOW DRAG

Song: Cat Scat

Cat scat cat scat
Ba dat ba dat
You say
Ba dat ain't love
Ba dat ain't love
The way you look at cat scat
Dat be dat infatuation
Can't be love
Can't be satisfaction
Dat be dat rap rapture
Dat sappy do dat
It ain't love
If cat a street rat
Be dat hustlin cat
Be dat fat pockets cat
Be dat cat wit
Permanent plaits
No Dax

Dat bad cat
Dance wit death
Git in quick spats
War gash on his back
Be dat cat scat
Wit rap to snap
Yo back
& daughter
Dat cat too black
Too much attitude
Dat cat like to slack
Cat scat lyrics
Cat keep you fat
Like dat like dad like Daddy
But Mama no flack
He be dat rat a tat tat
On my window
He got me doin mathmatics
Be dat slick cat tap dancin
On my bare black back
You got me
Cat wit
Permanent plaits

5 South 43rd Street, Floor 2

Sometimes we would get hungry for the neighborhood.
Walk up the sidewalk towards Chestnut Street.
Speak to the Rev holding the light-skinned baby,
ask his son to come put a new inner tube on my bike.
Cross Ludlow, past the mailbox on the corner,
Risqué Video, Dino's Pizza, and the Emerald Laundromat.
The fruit trucks tucked into 44th Street on the left,
house eyes shut with boards, fringes of children.
Once we went into a store sunk into the street,
owned by a Cambodian woman. She sold everything,
from evening gowns to soup. Over to Walnut and 45th,
where the Muslim cat sells this chicken wrapped in pita,
draped in cucumber sauce. The pregnant woman
behind the counter writes our order out in Arabic.
We grab a juice from the freezer, some chips,
eye the bean and sweet potato pies.

Back into the hot breath of West Philly, sun is setting.
The sky is smeared squash, tangerines in a glaze.
Three girls and one boy jump doubledutch. A white man
hustles from the video store with a black plastic bag.
We look for money in the street, steal flowers
from the church lawn. The shit stain from the wino
is still on our step. Mr. Jim is washing a car for cash.
John is cleaning his rims to Buju Banton.
Noel is talking sweetly to the big blue-eyed woman.
Linda, on her way to the restaurant. The sister
in the wheelchair buzzes by with her headphones on.

One night, a man was shot and killed on this block,
right outside our thick wood door. But not today.
Today is one of those days to come home from walking

in the world, leave the windows open, start a pot of
black beans. Smoke some Alice Coltrane. Cut up
some fruit, toenails. Hold on to the moment
as if time is taking your blood pressure.

SONG: WORTHY

They met on a Friday afternoon in Philadelphia
He was sharp with a New York walk
She was a suburb girl with a sailor's mouth

Typewriters her Fortune 500
A double bass was all he owned
But they made a crib out west
The center of their universe

Worthy, worthy
Worthy of the richest love
They were worthy, worthy
Worthy of the blackest love

Deeper than Iraqi oil
Darker than Belgian chocolate
More opaque than midnight sky
More comely than Sheba

She saw fingers wrought for good fortune
Locks like the tallest trees
He took her thighs for hymns & mantras
Her scars for heirloom jewelry

While the world was runnin amuck
Chasin gold, diamonds & land
They were content to sip each other's skin
& savor their souls

Worthy, worthy
Worthy of the richest love
They were worthy, worthy
Worthy of the blackest love

Deeper than Iraqi oil
Darker than Belgian chocolate
More opaque than midnight sky
More comely than Sheba

Between "Django" and "The Thrill is Gone"

you melt my melancholy dew
my bop canyons licked clean
my heavy girl mouth
draped with your kisses
you disarm me with the traffic
light of your musk
you blow your horn and cause
an ancient accident
between these nipples
with each thrust of your
steamboat romance
you exert something over me
you make something rise
under my cheeks
you are the rose pressed
between these bible belt legs
if I could hit a high note
for every epiphany you rustle in
in my bush and briars, every
rake you run through my dread,
I'd make opera
out of the bygone eras
in your eyes
I'd make Mayan empires
shiver with ruin
coming out of your pores
I'd thrill you
with this voice
that wells up
to say your name

SONG: DIDO

Mandingo
Grew up in the Bay of
Montego
Child of martyrs said he'd
Rather be my hero
Re-invent me in the coves of
Montenegro

Bilingual
He altered the way of
My lingo
His tongue had a style so
Instinctual
Untied my vines &
Bewitched my mango

High
The road he took to
Slay all my doubts

Slow
His maneuvers to
Eat my heart out

Mandingo
Is my cure
Like Frida's Diego
I love him for reasons
Beyond ego

FROM ALBERT'S STUDIO

on our way
back from Risqué Video

giggling all
over Greene Street

we found a black and white photo
dated March 29, 1947
on the back: "Albert's Studio,
1928 South Street"

a black nun
no, a Muslim woman

she reminded me
of someone

looking up at me
on the sidewalk
felt her reaching

left her
on a stoop

said
take care of yourself

later

we watched porn
and smoked Buddha

I forgot
her face

some things you find
are not for you
to keep

HEATHER WORE HER SADNESS

Heather wore her sadness like a brooch on her lapel
Joyce wanted to birth her baby naturally
Rita said she got pregnant doing it upside down
Carla loved to dance for basketball players
Hilary knew how to make garlic bread
Gloria wore her thick braid tight round her skull
Fay wandered with cigarettes and iced tea
Malvia a primrose far from birth, morals of concrete
Shawn let her hair drink henna and mayonnaise
Gwen taught me about wearing murderous shoes
Sonia reminded me about cotton underwear
June made a fancy restaurant into a soul shack
Tanya painted pictures holy enough for churches
Heather wore her sadness like a brooch on her lapel

English Department Meeting Query

1) What is cultural tension? What are some examples that we see in the world, in our neighborhoods, in our school?

The working class guy named Jim next door
with his bumper sticker about Unions and his
shit about Puerto Ricans. His nosy Buddhist
wife, hands in the cookie jar of the earth.
A little brood walking from the
pool in summer, cussing up a storm down
Morris Street. Black Miss Barb inquiring like their
grandmother but being shunned, "Shut up, bitch."
The look I sometimes get w/locks: Shampoo
questions in frowns, affirmation in nods.
The smell of Abyssinia + Pearl of Africa
on South Street. The Latino shop owners,
the boys who tell them "Suck my nigga candy."
The white boy on the corner assaulted at sea,
drowning in learned coolness. The multi-colored
family next door. The moment when an old black man
said to me we as a people weren't okay. The moment
when an old black barber in his white coat asked for
a taste before I married. The sista who looked crazy at first,
stepped out of her fog and said, "You right. Good for you."

SONG: ARTEMIS' BLUES

Hunt for me in the shade
Please me with sunsets
Make no tears
Fall from me, dear
Don't make no apologies
That sway like mythologies

Hunt for me in the shade
Tempt me with moonshine
Pour it slow
I aims to swallow
Then hang the silver pitcher
On the little big dipper

Hunt for me in the shade
Amuse me with seasons
Turn the planet dial
I'll oblige for awhile
Make my winters merciful
& my summers ethereal

Don't bring no weapons
Just bring yo person

Hunt for me in the shade
Don't be stingy wit yo fire
Intentions understood
Baby be my Prometheus
Let the gods quarrel beneath us

There's a tree I frequent
When the air get sharp
Look for me round de ben
Where shadows stalk the dark

Don't bring no weapons
Just bring yo person to
Hunt for me
Hunt for me

III   HARRIET

SONG: MELON RAP

Cantaloupe ain't nothin
But some kind of handmedown
When you can have a

Water watermelon
Red lips beady eyes
Everytime I eat you
Got to wear a good disguise

Can't indulge in public
Folks might call me coon
So I grow you in my backyard
By the dull light of the moon

Spit one seed black
Mouth be all red
They say the big green basin
Be a nigga's deathbed

Still cantaloupe ain't nothin
But some kind of handmedown
When you can have a

Blood red melon
Proper folks sigh
But if I can't have you
Part of me dies

American Valentine

I. *"Slave Poet's 1776 Letter, 'New Discovery,' Is for Sale"*
    —*New York Times*, November 11, 2005

Phillis to Obour,
Valentine's Day 1776.
Her lacerating ink
worth $253,000.

In eight years
she will die broke,
but here
she slashes out
pulpit with pen
to sister-friend,
knows a thing or two
about BARBARITY, EVIL
and CRAFTINESS,
and still talkin bout REVOLUTION,
American as the LIBERTY
on her tongue
of Latin-edged lingo.

They sayin
this paper holy grail,
and yeah, this our birthright,
being black and writer.
Phillis speaks to us
across auction and museum,
sings the GOSPEL,
puts it all in
the big man's hands.

Look how the "P" curls
like the hook
of a Christmas ornament.
Look how she's
carved out a piece of
DOMINION for us
to sup on, our own
dreamy continent
to idle in,
her purple "X"
on the white sheet
of English Lit.

II.

why do I keep returning
to Miss Phillis
who used to be a sellout
who used to dance
that waitress two-step
that shuffle?

she was a first love
I sniffed the peonies
under her starched verses
and fingered the cornrows
under her waspy bonnet
and she cooed for me
gushed metaphorically
till we were both spent
but not sold

my Phillis
who got served
with the slave's
not the poet's
destiny

III.

kind white
women
her gurus.
her source of
coddling
cobbling.
glovéd hands
arranging
for a trifle
her parts,
tiny barbs
for a music
box.

IV.

when I was seven
I knew the smell
of my mother
was part Lauren
part herb
part turbinado

no one in Boston
nor at Harvard

could teach
her the elegiac forms
of Wolof
the metered grief
of an African mother
no one to cross-
examine her
on the riddle
of her real name

the schooner
birthed her
and filled her memory
with water

V.

I used to believe
the fairy tale
of Phillis
the flower that
should have never
been uprooted,
never survived,
an intellect
too frail
to be transplanted
without constant
heat and light,
the girl
who learned to
live in an incubator
of whiteness,
her husband

the wolf
who pillaged
the rare crop
the Wheatleys had cultivated.

Then I fell in love
with a free man.

VI.

riverine woman
wolverine woman
tambourine woman
Byzantine woman
Maybelline woman
magazine woman
libertine woman
evergreen woman
Springsteen woman
mangosteen woman
mezzanine woman
Benvereen woman
jujubean woman
aquamarine woman
velveteen woman

HARRIET

I.

he hit
Ol' Harriet
in the head.
her head sure
did ache.
but a hundred
blacksmiths sprung
from her dome and wove
a cage of resistance
round her body.
that's what
made her strong.
blacksmiths descended
from real Africans
who knew
the secrets of iron.
alchemic dervishes.
like Sam Johnson's
faeries, they stayed
close to their beloved
after that master assault.
did she know they existed?
did she take advantage
of their power?
only the lynching oak
and freedom-killing swamp
would know.

II.

she was always ugly.
rough on the eyes.
look like a daughter of Ham.
but her inside-flesh
was green as lime.
inside out,
she would have been
a concubine
or goddess
or a rainforest
plant possessing
hermetic properties,
but she did not learn
that inside-out trick
till she was free.
the first time.
she learned
by watching folk
who'd been free awhile.
they stopped looking
backwards.
she learned
when the hand,
elegant as a leaf,
brushed her thigh
and made the gingham
in her lap
blush.

III.

Harriet,
I pine
for your courage.

the jaguar voice
you used sparingly.

should my mouth
run over
with kitten phrases,
I practice
your genius
of survival,
study your paradigm
swift, mark the way
you created
your own office
out of shade
and dusk.

Harriet,
I dream
to sleep
in your musk
of many
thousands gone.

IV.

how do you move
a people
through time?
you can write a song
you can do a dance
but your star
stands still and fades.

Harriet made a way
out of her own way
she did not tell herself no, can't
she was made
of the ice
at the head
of the comet,
not the dust
spiriting behind.

the trees
were her lovers
the wet earth
her alibi
she knew the way
forward
was going back
and she gathered
us up.

V.

I make a séance
of her birth name
Araminta
ancestor who
delivered us
from Eden

so invoke her
when they belittle you
push you to the fringes
of your own city

invoke her
when you're feeling
like a credit score
bent and bleeding
from this American
cat's toying

perhaps
she will surge
through you
like a drug
and you will feel her
in your tongue
burning between
your lips
with the fury
of flight

VI.

A dredwoman
Is an unkept woman
A free woman

Nappy-limbed woman
Body & soul undomesticated
Suspicious, profiled woman
On the run to emancipation

Supreme gardener
Lynch line retracted
Beauty found dung-deep
Nuclear war extracted

Gurglin black plumes
Cables to rage
Delphic fleece
Envelopin Osage

Vertigo tightly rolled
Mine-free crown
Respect in the head nod
Walkin round town

With her hair like wanderlust
She is unbound

With her hair like a cipher
She is bloodbound

From Imhotep's Kundalini

what thoughts I have of you tonight, Du Bois
of bodies rocked and minds embalmed in bark
our blanched arrival—seethin with scandal's mark
nowadays I peep you in the bean-pie seller's poise

with that silhouette fit for bust or cameo
I can't always divine your debonair birth
or your boocoo brain laborin like an earth
in hallelujah's ether, somehow duckin death's blow

sure sprung from Imhotep's kundalini
stitchin white reconstruction's funeral shroud
scriptin Philly dirges for the cryin out loud
cussin Garvey's name over martinis

sometimes I wonder if you double agent on the page
or mastermind of our ordered rage

SONG: AFRICAN IN NEW YORK

Malian blood-beans in your coffee, dear
Congo diamonds on your bride
Taste the Cape of Good Hope in your lemon
A little bit of Africa in New York

My bones are buried neath Fifth Avenue
My spirit haunts the Upper East Side
You see me lurk in every corner
Little bit of Africa in New York

I'm an African, I'm a phantom African
Caught in cosmic limbo in New York
I'm an African, I'm a phantom African
Talkin that cosmo lingo in New York

Color maketh man in life and death
The ink of history fades away
Takes a spook like me to change your hairstyle
A shadow of yourself, conjured by the day

I'm an African, I'm a phantom African
Caught in cosmic limbo in New York
I'm an African, I'm a phantom African
Talkin that cosmo lingo in New York

America, you beautiful suitor of indigenous bitches. I am a slaveship and you are a skyscraper. I keep the bottom line, you got the upper hand. We try to make love but there's a war of flesh and steel going on.

Used to woo me with roses carved from melons, douches of Colt 45 and holy water, ivory pearls that turned out to be my grandpa's wisdom teeth. I must have been crazy to keep setting your place at the welcome table, thinking this or that would be the night that you eat from my fork of blues. Said you loved me but you just loved my doggy style. You ejaculated rotted dreams, rusted passion across my chest. In the morning, you left my thighs like crackbrained riverbeds, left the scent of your hunger in my hair.

Ashamed to say I fell in love with you, America. With your swagger and your big talk. Nobody told me your heart was the world's first digital camera, beating humanity into bloody squares. Nobody told me how you cut mugs from the get-go, the army of hookers you ran with before you lay in my bed, the arsenal of whips and ropes in your closet for the cowboy flicks you produced, directed, and starred in every century.

You keep telling me how you different now, you saved. But you keep making purple moons rise on my eyes. Say you sorry but you still find a way to 302 me into oblivion. Build me a dollhouse of steel cages so all my flowers can grow separate and evil. Laugh like a tree grinder when you read my suicide letters. From my soul you make a sharecropper, a little black box.

America, I am the slaveship and you are the skyscraper. I keep the bottom line, Baby, you got the upper hand. We makin love and there's a war of flesh and steel goin on. America, you the most sublime, transcendental fornicator. You keep gettin caught with your dick out, tryin to drill a hole in the world. Sometimes I wanna fuck you like there is a tomorrow and a tomorrow and a tomorrow. Sometimes I wanna take your hand, take you to the little markets where the people sell their spirits in small pieces, to the alleyways the hustlers have made soft with hip talk. Walk hand-in-hand along a beach unbought and unbridled, and ride you till you say my name and you change, change. You'd brand me with invisible kisses. I'd be just like those talk-show mamas—forgiving. We'd meet every day at the intersection, the bridge, the phone booth, the hot dog stand, and you'd tell me your baby dreams, the ones dense and wet as first forest. Show me your dirty drawls and your secret birthmark. Maybe then, America, I might give myself to you.

SONG: DOZENS

You knock yourself out
But you just a hair on Muhammad Ali's fist
Ain't even no fighter

All your jokes die slow deaths
In the ring of my roses

Watch out, cuz I'll shame you
Your knockers popped out
Like Janet's in every round

How could you begin to faze me
You ain't dynamite, baby, you dyspepsia.

Your mouth is a bandwagon
Without wheels
Your spine is a double-dutch rope
Twirled by a double-handed doofus
Your style is a mouse-chewn tootsie roll

& your talk is George Foreman
But I'm the greatest butterfly
Weavin crop circles
On yo mamaland

NOTES FROM A SLAVE SHIP

At the end of heavy breathing,
at the beginning of grief and terror,
on the X2, the bus I call a slave ship.
The majority of its riders BLACK.
Pressed to journey to Northeast,
into voodoo ghettos
festering on the knuckles
of the "Negro Dream."

—"Heavy Breathing," Essex Hemphill

"Time does not change us. It unfolds us."
—Sign in front of church on H Route

57, Rising Sun and Fisher

picture of a slave ship
in a social studies textbook
bodies crammed
sardines among sardines
black stick figures
on every inch. intimate
storage. UPS love.
spatial revenge. Feng
Shui heresy. one
semen. one stream.
one urine. one menarche.
one shit. one breath.
the bodied ship
the ship of breasts
legs, orifices like
portholes

this city is a kind of
ocean
North Philly flotsam
adrift. we mangle
one another with glances
don't dare touch.
branded with other ship names
in the newer world:
Abercrombie and Fitch
Lucky Brand
Gucci
Louis Vuitton

Broad and Goree

all this stirrin
slow cookin
chicken fryin
babies cryin
niggas smokin
bitches waitin
junkies stalkin
con men walkin
deals breakin
Buddha scratchin
Allah rappin
Christ jumpin
dashikis sellin
XH lurkin
53 delayin
56 repeatin
sistas draggin
jeans bucklin
strollers rollin

daycare closin
barbers groomin
devils loomin

53, Wayne and West Abbottsford

black sweatshirt
smooth lips
hard brother
mouthing words
parting
at the bus stop
on Wayne Ave

I can't hear you
but the words are
warm in her ear
you're on the sidewalk
she's on the first step
looking back
and the rest of us
are waiting to move again

behind you
in the mist
behind the courts
brothers sit
on a park bench
in a New Jack moment
I imagine they are
having the sagacious
conversation
of accomplices
or lovers

and when she's
safely boarded
you scan
this vessel
for criminals
and walk away

her hoodie
is pink

when she sits
I notice the barrette
in her hair

J, Belfield and Wister

cornrows
why you gotta
tear your boy down
in front of us
tellin him
not to be a snitch
when he gets off the bus
tellin him
to say
somethin else
say somethin
go head
his head hangs
my heart breaks
maybe he is a bad boy
what kind of life
you leadin him to?

a schoolgirl with dusty braids
rolls her eyes
your a.m. scoldin
cramps all our styles
on the shore white men
fondle our babies
breakin back after back

aboard here
we are our own masters
can only control
the minutes &
our baby mouths

Broad Street Line, City Hall

these ruts come & go
buildin like nausea
round my flo
pale bitches wanna step
I cut their hair, give em strep
& weave whiplash
into their tongues
leave em botoxed & far flung
celebrity culture beckons
but who got time for Beckhams
I'm ridin Septa into Market East
keepin my shit clean, free of yeast
pushin a zone 4 trizzy
I can go anywhere in the city
ain't yo biddy, don't need yo pity
drama on the brain
sistas wearin tight jeans in pain
smokers light it up in the doorway
who's gonna start my day?

Postcard from Germantown to West Africa

arrived on a bus called
the 23
and shocked to find
no cowries but trolley tracks
on the long snake
they call Germantown Avenue.
wish I could be there
but I'm stuck in the New World
somewhere between Goree
and Coney Islands, a rollercoaster carrying
smallpox and a covered wagon full of
Uzis. The Cake Place, Lightning Beauty Supply,
Sound of Germantown say hello.
wish you were an Africa medallion round my neck
leather binding
the red, black and green sun that sets and rises
within our solar plexus.
kiss the pyramids and trap doors of history
for me. give my love to the sea bottom and the sharks.

XH, Broad and Erie

when I say you my nigga
I say it with more love
than anyone who's ever said it
in the world

when I say you my nigga
it suffices to say
that the utterance
is mutiny

against controversies and censors
none of which can erase
the black we share and suffer
I adore its uncircumcised edges
its lack of forgiveness

a vulnerable boy of a word
a bastard with the nerve
to have pride
inconceivable and blind
as a rocket ship
boyword that outlives
the crack of history

what they hungry to hate
heavy with wings they built
you still my nigga
more than theirs

Broad Street Line, Spring Garden

"...for the slaves lie in two rows, one above the other on each side of the ship, close to each other, like books upon a shelf."
        —John Newton, slave-ship captain between 1747 and
          1754. *Thoughts Upon the African Slave Trade* (1787)

what would I do to you
to get out of this funk
this ark of flesh

would I strangle you
as I suffocate
could I avoid your touch

would I forget
my child
in the madness of a mad itch
that will not cease
would I go mad mad mad
in a white-hot way

we forget ourselves
living in filth
living in hate
living in despise

Definition of a Slave Ship

one who
carries
goods
from one
world to

the next,
space pirate
father ship
devil frame
sorrow sonnet
ocean sieve
rowing volcano
bowl of cherry pits

IV   MONK EATS AN AFRO

SONG: PIC NIC

Pic a chic
No nic a nigga
Nic him in the leg
Eenie meenie him
Go holla head
& beg

Pic a nigga
For pickin
Tryin to be slick wit
A white chic

Kick cut dick
Make his mama sick
Let the sun
Lick the wounds

Pic a nic
Sittin in a tree
Don't neglect
To pick a pubescent nic
Not nearly shiftless
Think he free

Nic wit quick lips
Pig do that
Click click bang thing
See if the juice
Be bloody
& the seeds
Sing

RUBY FLO

some folks like to plug her up
but she's the only thing I can count on

queen of
solitude
repose
tranquility
assurance
she do that shit alone
& perfect
complete

you gotta let her be
& love her

what a comedian when she late
what a trickster when she early
what an actress when she heavy & dramatic
what a child when she light & free

my girl
crimson layers
honeyed with fruitfulness
scented with prebirth musk
unfoldin one after the other
out of this delta called
girl & then woman
then mama

she be fertility
La Baker sweat
Shug Avery pee

hooded & cloaked in red
reminiscent of the dawn after an eclipse
Chaka Khan's laden carmine lips
singin "Stay"

I like it when she come
red ridin in the night
quick on her feet & just-a-stealin
other times she ease right out of me
real slow like a juke joint song
a Tony Brown tune
hummed even & low
so you know she there

brazen &
sassy smellin
funky & fresh
my babymakin stew
only secret lips get to taste
answer all my questions
hush all my doubts
I ask her
how comes I git so low sometimes?
& she say

cuz I makes you still &
you gots to be still to hear
what you doin good
& not so
makes you interact
with all the stuff you don't need
& then helps you get rid of it
no need for cryin, agitatin or fussin
girl, don't fret these waters
they'll never drown you

I be that magic called creativity
the potion that made you
the fluid named passion in your pen
I'm the only ink been round since the beginnin

I be the ruby flo
I be the ruby flowin
that jewel
anciently
aggravatin
undulatin
explodin like a sunburst
inside you
& fallin out of you like
weary petals droppin
to the earth
seekin
rebirth

Lullaby at Seven Months

I have this feeling
that my heart will break
from the knowing of you
so every day
I will hold myself
to the fire of love
and sing you the lullabies
of my dreams
and even as I hold you
I will divine and fashion
my heart for the letting go
imagining space without
your scent, your newness
I will send the ashes of all
the ghosts who threatened our feast
to the winds that run counter
and I have this feeling
that the deepest cracks in my heart
will be cemented with joy.

Dawn in East New York

Mark tells me of taking an old girlfriend
in high school home early mornings before
school. Rising at 4:40am when even
the crackheads are asleep. The rising of
the sun like the filling of a cup with
orange juice. The city on inhale before
rush hour exhale. Driving down
tree-lined streets, the sound of birds
foregrounded, the growl of the subway
on some magical ducking until the
jump off. My man loves sunrises
and sunsets, I see. He is a creature
of the senses. He has taken in so
much air in his 35 years. And now
lying in bed for the past three nights
he studies the manual of a Nikon F60
holding the camera in lamplight, getting
ready to take a morning portrait of
my belly full of his son.

DIANE

I heard it was
bad luck to attend
a funeral so heavy
but I went
to see you off
anyway
my body was full
of somebody
I didn't know yet

it was one of those
funeral homes
that used to be
a corner store
once I sat down
in the back
I remembered
your s-curl
always heavy
with pomade
and your smile
imperfect with crowns

as they wheeled you
to the front of the room
the sheet slipped away
and revealed a leg
as ashen as a burnt log
slim as a dead stem
a leg I knew you
would be ashamed of
a leg I knew you had

wrapped around a man once
the preacher said
spirit lived on
but I saw how
your leg had assimilated
and succumbed

Diane
do you know
they had you lying in a
cardboard box
covered in bedsheets
with tea-colored stains
did you see me
trying to block out
grief like a bouncer
or a daughter

I wanted to tuck you in
wanted to give you
my stomach swollen
with promise

Campo Del Cielo

my stomach like iron
ribbons of melanin
like a meteorite dropped from heaven
this baby be a broken piece of lava
descended from dark ether
and somewhere there is a planet
missing its sun
and he is drifting through
my insides, displacing bone
and ground I thought was unyielding
he is enacting quiet bubbles of dance
for all the children
who were never hurled
from a space above

SONG: EVOLUTION

Outside our imagination
In the evolvin spin of time
In this universe of utter blackness
We keep marchin
In this grand parade
Out of the dark
Out of history
Out of media
Into the streets
Oh yes, Mama, the streets
Marchin in our triangles
Of generations
On genealogical journeys
To find our place & nation
Where will I find a home?
Where lies the way to the truest self?
Mama says, Mama says
It's the nexus
Of Africa & your own
Rare essence

I'm the virtuous
I'm the blamed
I'm the yearnin
I'm the grave
I'm the lost cause

I'm the slave
I'm the tired
I'm the fast-ass
I'm the coward
I'm the bombast
I'm the preacher
I'm the dog
I'm the chickenhead
I'm the hog
I'm the pilot
Of this plane
Better drive it
Past the sugar cane
Past tobacco
Past Colt 45
Past the bling
Past the shuck & jive

Evolution

I'm the fallen
I'm the first
I'm the burden
I'm the has-been
I'm the shallow
I'm the deep
Steady walkin
In my sleep
Oh I'm greedy

Oh I'm starved
Always singin
Steady marchin
I am a band
Of Africans

Evolution

Always singin
You are my band
Of Africans

Evolution

Steady marchin
In this army
Beasts of burden

Evolution

Thelonious Naps

beauty
sleeping, your face
assumes the stone
cheek of Michelangelo's
boys, but oh your curls,
a righteous vibrato
beneath Augusta's or
Edmonia's thumb.

MONK EATS AN AFRO

it came out
on a silver platter
with a choice of two sides:
he chose the fist-handled pick
and Crème of Nature conditioner

a sprig of Minnie's baby-breath
nestled in the underbrush
the house sauce was
a shallow dish of pink oil

he cut it into four quarters
with a steak knife
spun each section
on the prongs of his fork
like an orange rubber planet until
on his plate there were
four thick cornrows

he gave one to me
one to the baby
dropped one to the shi tzu
under the table
and slid one into his pocket
with a magician's
sleight of hand

he blew coils into the cool soup
the baby blew back raspberries
soon I was scatting
when in walked Ella
so I just shut up and listened

as she stuck the leftovers
into her purse
where tiny blues singers
hotcombed them on a conveyor belt
into sheets of butter
with notes of bop

Love Is Like a Faucet

after Billie

these vitamin double ds
gonna put cows outta business.
these Sunday bests
if frozen would delight.
unpasteurized & untamed
they swing
in the hammock
of my torso.
they magnetize
my man's hands.
like a Wonder Woman blast
or a web of thunder from
Storm's wrist,
this cocktail
is nurturing napalm
manna dew, Pepto Bismol
for civilization.
you can't outwit these
aureolas.
these nipples are
necrophilia's enemy.
Coltrane couldn't blow
these tumescent tubas.
these are gourds
that'll make a shekere
obsolete,
make an eggplant
go pale.
these breasts
gonna put old Betsy

outta business
& send the men
with goats a-packin.
this love is like a faucet,
it turns on & on.

Gangsta Birth

it was a gangsta birth:
screw the epidurals & the pitocin
ain't give the ob the opportunity
to cut a C# in me.

birth balls like tumbleweed
midwife cowboys
for the shoulder dystocia
& grandmothers angular as zoot suits,
secrets of ancestry unfoldin.

it was a gangsta birth:
it was radical manual labor
militant nativity
Tubmanesque rebellion
from the white sheets
deliverance to a planet
of endorphins in a box
built out of nerve.

the space between each contraction
like African sleepin sickness,
motions of slave ships in these hips.
the most productive eight-hour day,
I wanted to play Stevie Wonder
but Wutang came instead—
caps in the ass, wily-haired
& ghetto-fed.

I was ballin
& didn't have no Nikes on,
only Jordans to cross.

I was gettin bent
but there was no smoke,

only coconut water
gurglin virgin,
only hormones
like beebread
from my own flower,
which I could not resist.

CORNROW SONG

I was born into Babylon
Orange dreads down my back like fire
Burned the hands of all who touched
Folks never got much too close

In my second life, I wore a bush
Carried bowls on it back in Kush
Pharaoh asked if he could put his hands in it
I said, "You best not touch my shit"

Third life, I stepped into a pyramid
Blasted off to Sun-Ra's space
Shaved my head & left a galaxy
Bald planet my scalp became

But fourth life, ghosts put me upon a ship
Sufferin burned my skin like lye
I tucked my language back behind my ears
& sang, "Tongue, oh don't you die

"Got a railroad in my hair
Got a railroad in my hair
Got a railroad in my hair
Fingers laid the tracks I wear"

ACKNOWLEDGMENTS

The author gratefully acknowledges the editors of the following
   publications and websites in which versions of these poems
   have appeared:

"Pea Song": *The Ringing Ear: Black Poets Lean South*, University
   of Georgia Press; *Pluck!: The Journal of Affrilachian Arts and
   Culture; Meridians*

"The Myth of Stew": *Lavanderia: A Mixed Load of Women, Wash,
   and Word*, San Diego City Works Press

"Sookie": *The Ringing Ear: Black Poets Lean South*, University of
   Georgia Press

"Violin to Fiddle": *Hanging Loose*

Song: Cat Scat: *Cave Canem Anthology IV*

"Between 'Django' and 'The Thrill is Gone'": *APIARY*

"Harriet," *Stand Our Ground: Poems for Trayvon Martin and Marissa
   Alexander*, Freedom Seed Press

"From Imhotep's Kundalini": *Hanging Loose, The Philadelphia
   Inquirer*, philly.com

Song: Pic Nic: *Meridians*

"Ruby Flo": *Cave Canem Anthology V*

"Monk Eats an Afro," "Love Is Like a Faucet," "Gangsta Birth":
   Hanging Loose

Cornrow Song: *Cave Canem Anthology VI*

GRATITUDE

Blood:
Mark, my NagChampaCowboy. Yvonda, my angel. Yvette
& Yshonda, my heart. Christine, Mary, Gladys & Evelyn, my
womenfolk on the other side. Freys, Johnsons, McGruders,
Jordans, Moores, Nunezes, Oliphants, Palacios, Winders, Wishers.

Guides:
Rex Ahene, Sylvia Carey, Mark Clark, Mrs. Delp, Thea Diamond,
Rachel Blau DuPlessis, Devonne Gardner, Bob Hershon, David R.
Johnson, June Jordan, Deborah Leibel, Dick Lourie, Joy Mangano,
Carolyn Micklem, Jena Osman, Julia Parker, Steve Parks, Harrison
Ridley, Jr., Francis Romano, Sonia Sanchez, Beth Seetch, Mr.
Slugg, Ian Smith, Charles Stahley, Lee Upton, Carolynn Van Dyke,
Kathie Walsh, Diana Waters, Suzanne Westfall, James Woolley.

Tribe:
Leah Anderson-Rhyens, Rich Breazzano, Ian Canefire, Carlos
Cheek, Michael Cirelli, Eisa Davis, Larry Fowler, Lance Gamble,
Ross Gay, Duriel Harris, Douglas Kearney, M. Nzadi Keita, Trapeta
B. Mayson, Cathleen Miller, Tracie Morris, Ewuare X. Osayande,
D. Ryva Parker, Meg Goldner Rabinowitz, Ursula Rucker, Tim
Shepherd, Karen L. Smith, Monnette Sudler, Omar Telan.

Communities:
Cave Canem, City of Philadelphia Mural Arts Program,
Germantown Poetry Festival, Germantown Friends School, Girls
on the Move, G-town Radio, Lafayette College, Miquon School,
Montgomery County Poet Laureate Program, Panoramic Poetry,
Poetry for the People Philly, Temple University.